An Encyclopedia of Fossils

Andrea Almada

Rigby

A Harcourt Achieve Imprint

www.Rigby.com
1-800-531-5015

Introduction

No one has ever seen a live dinosaur. Did you ever wonder how we know so much about them?

Sometimes when a plant or animal dies, parts of it remain and become very hard, or leave behind a print. These are called fossils. Scientists use fossils to learn about plants and animals that lived millions of years ago.

Amber

Small insects can get trapped in a sticky sap that comes out of evergreen trees. When the sap hardens, it becomes amber. An insect that is stuck in amber doesn't change. Today we can see how it looked a long time ago.

This is an insect trapped in amber.

B Bones

When some animals die, their bones sink into mud or sand that later turns into rock. When scientists find these bones, they put them together like a giant jigsaw puzzle. The bones help scientists learn a lot about how these animals looked and acted, even though the animals are not alive anymore.

Cast

Casts and molds are fossils. If you press your hand into wet clay, and it hardens in the shape of your hand, you have made a mold of your hand. If you fill the mold of your hand with a liquid that hardens, you could have a copy of your hand. This copy of your hand is a cast. Fossils of footprints can form this way in clay or mud.

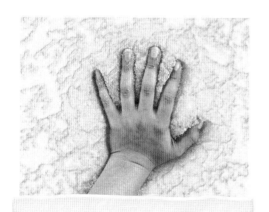

This is a mold.

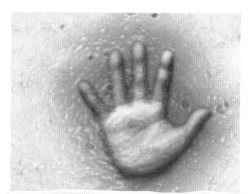

This is a cast.

D Dinosaur Valley State Park

At Dinosaur Valley State Park in Texas, you can see the footprints of animals that lived long ago. Dinosaurs made these tracks when they walked near rivers, on the shores, and through the mud.

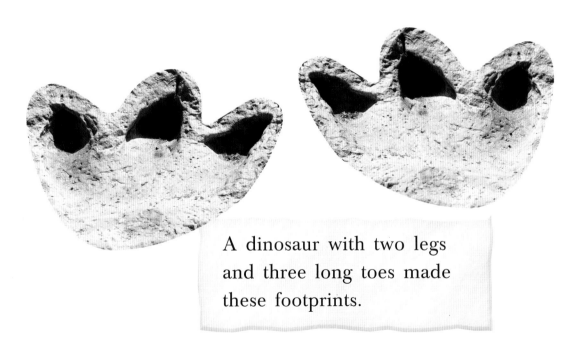

A dinosaur with two legs and three long toes made these footprints.

Scientists found fossils of dinosaur bones nearby. Then they matched the fossils to the footprints they found.

A dinosaur with two legs and bird-like feet made these footprints.

A dinosaur with four legs and round feet made these footprints.

 **Extinct**

If you look for a dodo bird, you won't find one. Dodo birds are extinct. This means that there aren't any of them alive now. Fossils give us clues that help us learn about extinct animals.

Fossil Fuels

Natural gas, coal, and oil are fossil fuels. They form deep in the ground from plant and animal remains. People use these fuels to cook food, drive cars, and heat their homes. Because it takes a very long time for these fuels to form in the ground, they cannot be replaced.

Ice

Ice is good for preserving animals. Millions of years ago, woolly mammoths in Siberia fell into ice holes and were trapped! The ground acted like a freezer that kept their bodies from rotting.

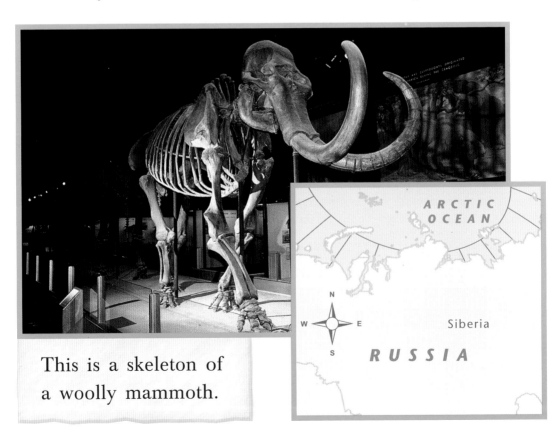

This is a skeleton of a woolly mammoth.

ARCTIC OCEAN

N
W · E
S

Siberia

RUSSIA

Scientists were surprised to find that woolly mammoths had fur, unlike today's elephants. Fossils were able to give scientists this information.

Jurassic Period

The Jurassic Period began more than 200 million years ago. Scientists have found many fossils from that time. Some of the fossils that they have found are from dinosaurs, lizards, flying reptiles, feathered birds, and very small mammals.

Fun Fact

Did you know that the Jurassic Period lasted 64 million years?

Limestone

Limestone is a kind of rock that often forms in the water. It usually has fossils because dead plants and animals sink to the bottom of the sea. When the mud hardens, the shells and bones become part of the stone.

Minerals

We find minerals in the ground. They are not plants or animals, and they were never alive. Water with bits of mineral in it can soak into a bone or a shell. When the water dries, it leaves the minerals behind. This forms fossils that are as hard as stone.

There are about 3,000 different kinds of minerals. Scientists sort minerals by their color, hardness, and shine. You can see different minerals when you look closely at a rock.

Fun Fact

Did you know that diamond is the hardest mineral?

O Ocean

When sea animals died long ago, their shells sank into the sand at the bottom of the ocean. Slowly the sand hardened, then became rock as time passed. Because the oceans have moved around over time, today we find fossil shells far from where they were formed.

These fossils formed at the bottom of the ocean.

P | Plants

Plants can become fossils. Many different plants left fossils of their leaves. We can see the shapes of very old leaves as we look at plant fossils.

A print on this rock shows a leaf shape.

17

S Saber-Toothed Cat

Scientists believe that fossils of some saber-toothed cats are 10,000 years old. The size of their bones tells us that the saber-toothed cat was bigger than the African lion. It had powerful claws and its teeth were 8 inches long.

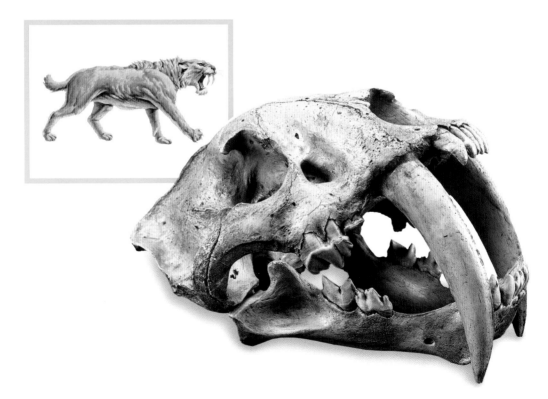

Shells

Millions of years ago, some seashells were filled with mud and water. Then the mud turned to stone. Because there were minerals in the muddy water, the shell fossils are the color of the minerals that turned them into stone.

Tar Pits

Tar is a very sticky black liquid. It comes out of the earth and forms gooey pools.

When animals got stuck in the tar, other animals tried to eat them. Before long, they were stuck, too. This explains why so many fossils are found together in tar pits. Scientists have found fossils of horses, bison, and other animals in tar pits.

Workers found these bison bones in a tar pit.

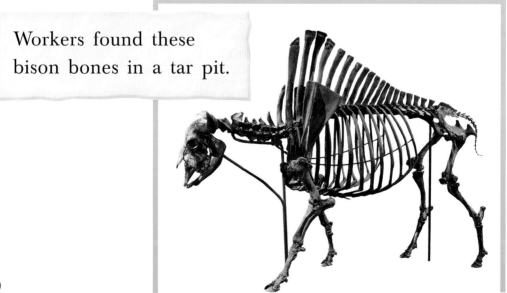

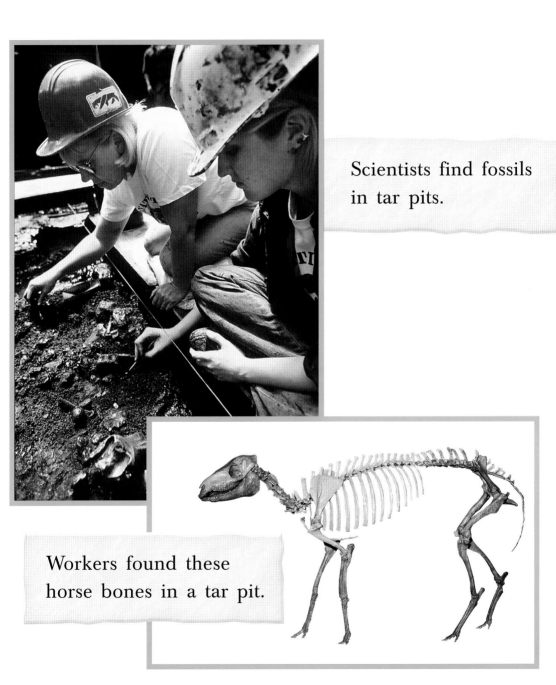

Scientists find fossils in tar pits.

Workers found these horse bones in a tar pit.

21

Tools

Scientists use special tools to dig fossils out of the ground. Workers chip away soil or rock around a fossil by placing a tool close to the fossil and tapping it gently with a hammer.

Once scientists remove a fossil, they use needles and brushes to clean it. Then they wrap the fossil and take it to a lab where they can study it.

Scientists carefully remove
fossils from the ground.

Wood

Wood can also become a fossil. When wood is covered by wet mud, clay, or sand, minerals seep slowly into the wood. When the minerals harden, the wood turns into stone. We call this petrified wood.

You can see petrified wood at the Petrified Forest National Park in Arizona.